THE BECOMING OF HER

DEZIANA TORRES

ISBN: 978-0-578-97233-6

DEDICATION

I dedicate this book to my younger self. The version of me that didn't believe in the potential to achieve the things I've accomplished today. In addition, to my higher self that leads me with courage and confidence.

I dedicate this book to my mother Carmen Castaner, the woman who sacrificed her own dreams to ensure that my siblings and I were able to reach our own.

To my siblings Jessica, Ysaira, Carmelyn, Raul, Jaylin, Ericka, and Ricky, I love ya till the death of me. You all and the babies are my motivation for everything.

Just as equally, I dedicate this book to you all, the ones who found value in my voice and dedicated time and energy to read the most vulnerable parts of me. May we all connect to this book in ways that inspires us to keep pushing for the dreams we wish to become our reality.

MSW GRAD PHOTOS TAKEN BY

NADIA ELHAWARY

TABLE OF CONTENTS

CONTENTS

Education

LOVE

Journal Entry

September 23, 2019

"Who am I outside my mask"

Deziana Torres, a woman who has been through so much trauma and heart-break. Since a little girl, I've sought to feel the love and affection I didn't receive growing up. I've searched to find this love in men who NOT only let me down but, broke my inner spirit. I am a woman who has so much pressure to be successful because I am the first in my family to achieve many things; utilizing opportunities my ancestors fought for me to have.

Truth is… I don't know what the fuck I'm doing. I am learning as I go and I am struggling to balance my school life, social life, friends, family, and self-care. I have experienced failures after failures and at first, I couldn't see the light within those days. But, now I learned to appreciate the lessons that came along with them. Although the mask hid my true emotions from the world, the wisdom learned is something I can't keep to myself. Although I found a way to shine in the midst of darkness, I too have my days.

So, who am I outside my mask? I am a just a human being who wants to heal from all the things that have impacted me. I want to wake up to peace and with the mental strength to control my thoughts when they become to self-destructive. I do not have it all together; I am convinced no one ever really does. I am willing to confront my inner demons, to tackle and heal from every trigger that arises because I know that through healing, rests a way better version of me.

The Becoming of Her

ACKNOWLEDGMENTS

The world is a better place today because since birth, I found a place of home with you. To the woman who taught me to see the good in people regardless of their bad, you kept me human. You taught me that people are products of their environments and if people had all that they needed to survive, then we'd live more peaceful lives.
People feel safe in my presence because you shared wisdom that allows me to hear the beat in people's hearts when pain lives inside. Listening to the stories they tell while, we watch them release what they kept buried alive.
Sugga mama, you live inside of my soul, I hope my legacy will forever show.

Carmen Milagros Lopez-Tello, (Grandma)
I acknowledge you for all you have instilled into my soul.

To the woman who watched me take my first breath and who I watched take her last.

A MESSAGE TO MY READERS

To those who took the time to invest and learn about my journey, I honor you and appreciate your entire existence. The purpose behind this book is to validate those who lived through similar traumas. To provide a moment of breath to those who silently struggle alone. The first step towards healing for myself, was to acknowledge and conquer my own triggers and their ties to my past, which kept me hostage in places of deep depression and anxiety.

My book will have some light poems to help refresh some good memories. Others, will teach you to reflect upon any triggering experience that may have altered the way you exist today. The ways in which we take advantage of moments to reflect, better prepares us for the work needed to bring forth the needed change.

The poems that can play as major triggers will have an "*" in the title. Please protect your peace if you aren't in the right head space for any triggers. It's okay to honor where you are.

After some of the poems, there are reflective writing activities that grant space for you all to reflect upon anything that came up when reading the poems. I challenge many to really take the time to write. There is power when a pen/pencil touches paper; believe me. To end the writing activity, you will find some breathing exercises to engage in followed by words of affirmation. My hope is to empower many to train your mind and body to become present in the moment again. The affirmations are a critical part of the book as they cancel any negative thoughts and replaces them with positive ones. Some of the affirmations you read, you probably won't believe and that is okay. It takes lots of practice which is why I intentionally wrote it for you to say it out loud four times.

We are individuals whose thoughts have the power to control our reality. My goal is that many of you learn to speak life into yourself and others around you daily. We live in a world that encourages hate and division and only love can conquer it all. Sounds simple, it's not. To reach a place to love safely and comfortably does take deep and painful inner work; we will get there together.

An internal transformation isn't always as easy as it looks. When you are reminded of any trauma and past hurts, you will remember why you kept it buried so deep inside. Be gentle with yourself in the process of healing. It will take time, consistency, tears, and support from others but, you are more than capable of getting the needed work done.

As long as there is breath in your body, there is purpose behind your life. I challenge you to remind yourself of this daily.

For many, trauma can linger and impact our ability to connect to ourselves and/or others. Most of us learned that talking about pain and struggles are considered a weakness so, as a result, we swallow down these heavy emotions and keep our struggles to ourselves. We assume we are alone but, truth is, many of us are just afraid to speak up.

By the end of this book, I want you to know one truth, that even if you have experienced a handful of failures, neither of them are strong enough to define YOU. Many of us made poor choices seeking comfort, or anything to fill the voids we felt in our lives. Starting today, like right now in this moment, we will no longer run from our pain. We will learn to cope in healthy ways, learn to better communicate, and learn to be kind to all in the midst of it all.

I encourage all to speak to a professional mental health specialist if you want to seek guidance with interventions that can specifically assist you on your journey towards healing. If you can't afford therapy, I encourage all to find creative ways that you personally enjoy, to help you release the pain that lives within. I'll share tips at the end of the book.

INSTRUCTIONS FOR THE BREATHING ACTIVITIES

- Step 1: Read the affirmation out loud
- Step 2: Close your eyes (if you are comfortable)
- Step 3: Breathe in (inhale) deeply for three seconds
- Step 4: Breathe out (exhale) slowly for three seconds
- Repeat steps 1-4

Ready to give it a try?

"I WILL FACE MY FEARS COURAGEOUSLY TODAY"

Inhale deeply. Exhale slowly. Now say the line above

Repeat 4x

INTRODUCTION

The Becoming of Her began in the midst of engaging in deep shadow work during the global pandemic. Shadow work is known to confront the parts of ourselves that we hide the most. In my shadow, I hide my insecurities, my pain, my struggles, and everything else that brought me shame, guilt, and all those unwanted heavy feelings.

I began to vulnerably share some of these struggles on my social media page and this is what sparked for the existence of this book. People who I had never met before, were reaching out to me to express how my posts were validating to the hidden pain they too suppressed. I mean a lot of people. These souls would instantly begin to reflect upon the triggers that arose for them from my posts and together, we'd exchange in storytelling and would find peace in knowing that we weren't alone in these common adversities. How could it be, that my life experiences that were heavy in guilt and shame also held power to validate and inspire others?

This book moves intentionally to provide the same space to all readers who are interested in confronting their own triggers in order to discover alignment and purpose.

The book is broken down into four categories; Childhood, Education, Love, and Self-love. All four sections play a major role in the way I exist and advocate today. In each section, understand that it is my story I am telling. Maybe you have experienced something similar but, had a different outcome or impact, that's normal. The beauty in life is that we are all uniquely different in how we experience even the things that are commonly struggled with.

In each category, I hope that you are able to challenge yourself in ways that push you to reflect upon your own triggers. When a trigger arises, I learned that it was best to recognize it, reflect upon it, challenge it, and heal from it. The tips I share at the end of the book may/may not work for you, that is also okay; try them anyways. This book aims to inspire many to begin to self-discover themselves and attend to their own personal needs. For any tips and tools that are successful, I encourage you all to add them into your daily routine and to be consistent with them. This is key to the becoming of the greatest version of yourself.

CHILDHOOD

The moments in our lives that hold weight to shape and control the way we exist in adulthood.

Birthdate

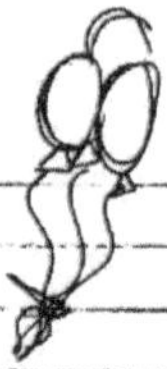

I was born female to teen parents
who confidently assumed I was male — ?
you see,
ultra sounds back then weren't accurate
so, they relied on the wisdom
from the older generations
to prepare themselves as first time parents

Baby shower was full of colors like
green and Blue
and once born
I wore nothing But "boy" clothes
like onesies with footballs too

unnamed for a week
my existence was something no one was
prepared for . . .
yet, now
it's something the world always seeks
A force so strong and intentional

A gift to the world.
my light is MULTIDIMENSIONAL!

Deziana
TORRES

Birthdate

I was born female to teen parents who confidently
assumed that I was male
Ultrasounds back then weren't accurate
So, they relied on the wisdom from the older
generations
To prepare themselves as first time parents

Baby shower was full of colors like green and blue
And once born
I wore nothing but "boy" clothes for months
Like the onesies with the footballs too

Unnamed for a week
My existence was something no one prepared for
Yet now, it is something the world always seeks

A force so strong and intentional
A gift to the world
My light is multidimensional

Birthday

December 27th,
The day I once grew to hate

in between holidays,
There's NVA enough room
to celebrate,

friends rarely ever showed up
during my planned events

and I know that if I died,
more people would show up to honor my death

It's been proven
time and time again

crazy how we "valve" those around us
in ways we always learn to
regret. ⟶

Birthday

December 27th
The day I grew to hate

In between Holidays
There's never enough room to celebrate

Friends rarely ever showed up during my planned events

And I know that if I died, more people will show up to honor my death

Crazy how we "value" those around us
In ways we always,
Learn to regret

Happy Birthday Deziana!

Oatmeal

Sugga Mama used to wake us up at 6:00am
Playing records that made our hips
Do twists and dips in our sleep

That Puerto Rican rhythm
Hits different in the morning
Singing,
"Time to clean"
Without words that speak

We'd creep out the rooms
Sugga would hand me a broom
Immediately, I'd sweep

As a reward,
She taught me to cook for myself
She grabs oats & milk
Then,
Sugga pours sugar in the pot
And kisses me on the head
Until it is no longer hot

I miss her bowls
of this sweet and special meal

Ouuuu
I love me some of Sugga's good,
Oatmeal

REFLECTIVE WRITING ACTIVITY

What memories (if any) arose about your grandparents? If your grandparents have died, what would you say to them if you could talk to them again?

Reflect on the questions above.

"I AM GRATEFUL FOR ENRICHED MEMORIES"
Inhale deeply. Exhale slowly. Now say the line above
Repeat 4x

Bullets and Playgrounds

By: Deziana Torres

Ever played at a park in the
heart of the hood?

my favorite one was on coolidge Ave
A park that only a few
could withstand

There's more than swings and slides
like shootings and drive bys

so we'd play over bullet shells
on pavements where bodies fell

"Tag"
"you're it"

Thoughts that came up when writing this..
• why are parks so dangerous for our kids in the hoods? How can we come together to start ensuring neighborhood accountability safety?

~~in other words,~~ what do we gotta do to create safe spaces for our youth to exist and play w/o the violence?

Bullets and Playgrounds

Ever played at a park in East or West Oakland?
My favorite one was on Coolidge Ave
A park that only a few could withstand

There's more than swings and slides

Like shootings
and drive-bys

So, we play over bullets shells
On pavements
Where bodies fell

Tag!!
You're it!

*Unhealed Parenting

As the oldest, I watched two unhealed souls
Hurt each other unintentionally

Loving in ways they've only experienced
Teaching me to love in the ways they taught

A cycle
So familiar
It can make my body shiver

Domestic violence
Cheating
& Broken promises

No wonder love for me
Was full of constant darkness

Unhealed parenting
Is quite life threatening

So, heal now
Before your children are forever left wondering,

'Does love even really exist?"

REFLECTIVE WRITING ACTIVITY

Who in your life influenced how you give love? Were the behaviors you learned considered healthy or toxic? How is your ability to love impacted by these behaviors when you began dating?

Reflect on the questions above.

"I AM DESERVING OF SAFE AND HEALTHY LOVE"

Inhale deeply. Exhale slowly. Now say the line above

Repeat 4x

*Single Parent Household

Dark divorce left my mother with four hungry children
An adversity we faced that was intentionally hidden
And as the eldest,
My responsibility was quite different

Cook and Clean'n at the age of nine
Watching a woman who was only twenty-five
Struggle to feed and help her children survive

I'd hear her crying alone on her bedroom floor
I stood silently on the other side of the door
Confessing with her mouth, she whispered

"I can't do this… anymore"

So, I'd get up to clean the house
Hoping she'd see that she didn't need another spouse

& later that night, a little past midnight
I woke up out of my sleep & felt the urge to emit light

She sat crying alone in her car
She had just taken an entire bottle of pills,
A plan so critical, she was ready to give it all up

"Mommy are you okay?"
In silence,
She clenched her soul and prayed

"Lord I change my mind, I can't leave my kids
PLEASE...PLEASE let me make it another day"

REFLECTIVE WRITING ACTIVITY

Write about the struggles that existed for you in a single parent household. If you had both parents, express if both were attentive to your everyday needs.

Reflect on the questions above.

"I DESERVE TO LIVE"
Repeat 4x
National Suicide Prevention Lifeline
Hours: Available 24 hours. Languages: English, Spanish.
800-273-8255

*Childhood Trauma

Age six,
The blood-stained carpet held a close relationship
with my mother and father
His anger was released from his fists and forced upon
My mother's body
A recreation of his own upbringing of being raised in a
broken home

Age eight,
Familiar hands touched sacred places
Silence sealed my lips
When he placed his hand over my mouth
And whispered,

"If you scream...I'll touch your sister next"

Age thirteen,
Mama is a single parent
30 years old without a diploma,
With a low wage paying job,
and four hungry children

She'd ask,
"Should we have food this month or electricity?"
She didn't have a lot but, it was always enough

As the oldest,
Sacrificed my childhood
To help raise my siblings
My mama needed help

Age fifteen,
I found "Love."
For my definition of love
Was what I've witnessed growing up

I craved to be wanted
His fists would leave bruises
I wanted to feel loved
He insisted that I must please him
Sex was evil, I had not healed yet

Silenced love but, on social media
we were "goals" tho

Age 27
Healing and realizing the connection to love
Was deeply rooted in the way
I experienced it growing up

Don't be convinced by what you do see
Cuz I don't always show what lays beneath me

I am still in the process of healing
From my own childhood trauma

*Spanish Music

For twenty years,
I never understood why I found myself triggered
by Spanish music that was authentic in my culture

Until one day
I asked my higher self for a clearer vision
Then the trigger revealed itself

The Spanish music that my family loved so much
Reminded me of the man who stole my childhood
innocence

It played during our backyard events
That Spanish music silenced my lips

The screams hid like shadows
behind the speaker's hits

I was excited to realize
It wasn't a disconnect from my own culture
Instead,

My peace was stolen
By an evil and selfish vulture

REFLECTIVE WRITING ACTIVITY

Did a trigger come up for you? Identify the feelings and emotions associated with the topic of sexual abuse. Where on your body did you feel that?

Reflect on the questions above.

"I AM DESERVING OF PEACE"

Inhale deeply. Exhale slowly. Now say the line above

Repeat 4x

Sorry Mama

I'm sorry
For pushing men out of your life
The ones who saw you for your body,
Not your beautiful mind

Men that you taught me to never trust
Men that Sugga taught you to never depend on
For reasons Wela held so much distrust
Shit was generational

I was trained to protect you as a young girl
From all the witnessed trauma
of a man,
Who I watched beat the life out of ya

Can you imagine?
A baby girl watching that happen to her mama?

Oh, you can?...

So, I was a baby reflection of your own unhealed
trauma
Living prisoner to those hidden emotions
that you haven't had time to heal yet

It's okay, you gave it your all anyways

Sorry mama,
I didn't accept any man after that
And no, I wasn't trying to ruin your love life

I was scared of you ever being alone
To a man, who didn't deserve you as their wife

Jumbo Jack Without Cheese

With the suppressed pain,
That I carried as a young teen girl,
I forgot gratitude

In the drive through of Jack in the Box,
The only food we could afford around the first of the month
When rent and bills were due
My mama didn't have enough to feed herself
So, she'd pretend to not be hungry

She knows I hate cheese on my Jumbo Jack
To a point where I'd crumble one up in her face
and toss it into the trash,
Along with my respect

I was ungrateful
My mama made the request
"Can I get a Jumbo Jack without Cheese?"

I can hear the
"I'd whoop your ass if you were my daughter"
And you see, she would

But, I was numb to the pain
That already consumed me

My behaviors were a silent cry for help
Yet, I was seen as the troubled teen

Just remember,
Next time you order my Jumbo Jack
Make sure it's **always** without the cheese

"Bag lady"

my mother said that when she hears
the erykah badu's
"Bag lady" she always thinks of me

A lady carrying invisible baggage so heavy
it's noticeable

Baggage tied tightly around my tired back
as my hands drip blood carrying groceries
of the only things provided to me

Things that keep our stomachs
full of misery
oh, how heavy is that generational pain & trauma damn

so sad,
the bags would be handed down to ya
by your own mama — (still ♥ you mama)

walking into spaces of unknown healing
I am the well known "bag lady"
singing proudly
"I guess nobody ever told you."
"all you must hold onto..."
"is you"
"is "you"
"is youuu ouw"

I am a bag lady, soon to be the healed lady

Because I promise aint no one
carrying these bags after me.

Bag Lady

My mother said that when she hears
Erykah Badu's "Bag Lady," she thinks of me

A lady carrying invisible baggage so heavy
it's noticeable

Baggage tied tightly around my tired back
As my hands drip blood carrying groceries of the only
things provided to me

Things that keep our stomachs
full of misery

Oh, how heavy is that generational
pain and trauma
So sad, the bags would even be given to you
by your own mama

Walking into spaces of unknown healing
I am the well-known "bag lady"
Singing proudly

"I guess, nobody ever told you,
All you must hold onto
Is You,
is you,
is youuuu"

I am a bag lady
But soon, I'll be the healed lady

I promise, no one is carrying
these bags after me

Oaktown

I am Oakland's beauty and Resiliency
Moving in intentional ways that often screams
"Where is our liberty?"

I am Fruitvale Bart Station
Where Oscar Grant fought to live
Against a unit of oppression
Of racism and colorism

I am Fremont High School
Rich in REAL diversity
The one that is now no longer recognizable
Redecorated for the privileged kids

I am the bullets that missed the innocent
By inches this time
Granting them another day to live

I am the poverty that keeps our people hungry
Committing acts of robbery
To keep our stomachs from hurting

I am the victims of police brutality
That are harassed in our streets
Yea, we ain't perfect
But, we deserve more than the high rates
of mortality

I am the drugs that consumes the lives
of the most hurt
Running away from problems

That often leaves us in buried in the dirt

I am also the beauty that lives deep within
the cracked streets and bullet shells
Although life is hard here
We will never fail

I am the hope of success
Chasing dreams regardless of the emotions I
suppressed
Because where there is darkness
There is also a life that is blessed

I am the connected community
Always hustling to provide spaces of healing
and creativity

I am E14
The street that is always busy
With sideshows and bomb ass burritos to eat

You see,
Oaktown is a city
That raises the world's most
Memorable souls

Hyphy

more than a movement
where dreads, twists, and all heads shake

Hyphy,
The moves that "make the nosy
neighbors wanna call the cops"
"Hyphy"

~~something~~
A ~~word~~ TERM with too much meaning
than words could ever explain
"Hyphy"
A ~~term~~ Dance that the new karens
in our hoods could never attain

Hyphy
The "GO STUPID" "
"GO" "GO"
"Hyphy"
"Hyphy"
I swear, only the REALEST know

-Deziana
Torres

Hyphy

More than a movement
Where dreads, twists, and all heads shake

"Hyphy"
The moves that
*"Make the nosy
neighbors wanna call the cops"*

"Hyphy"
*A term with too much meaning
Than words could ever explain*

"Hyphy"
*A dance that the new Karens in our hoods could
NEVER attain*

"Hyphy"
The *"Go Stupid"*
"GO" "GO"
"Hyphy"

I swear,
Only the REALEST
From the Bay, know

Firework & Gunshots

I remember a monent when we were all
watching shrek for the 30th time
inside of cua's house in deep East Oakland
it was suaga's favorite movie

she would always laugh & call me Fiona
she was my Donkey

But as we watched, something so familiar
happened
shots rang and my siblings and I
always played the game.

A game where we had to guess if
the shots fired came from fire works or gunshots

my siblings and I all paused,
tried to recall the different vibrations
from each sound
when ready, we would count "one... two..." & on
three, we shouted our confident guesses
"gun shots"
we proclaimed then back to the movie
we went
"not my buttons, not my gumdrop
buttons"

The sirens sound surrounded the street
we all made eye contact
and high fived for being Right
But wait,
How did we get so good at this game?

Fire Works and Gunshots

(Short Story)

Watching Shrek for the 30th time
In deep East Oakland

Suddenly shots rang and my siblings and I always
played this game

A game where we had to guess if the shots fired
came from fireworks or gunshots

My siblings and I all paused,
Tried to recall the different vibrations from each sound

When ready, we would count "One…. Two…"
and on three, we shouted our confident guesses

"Gunshots," we proclaimed
Then back to the movie we went

"Not the buttons!!
Not my gumdrop buttons"

The sirens surrounded the streets

We all made eye contact
And high fived for being right

But wait,

How did we get so good at this game?

Gun Fight

My mama was a young adult
Who had more life to experience

When she'd go to the club
I'd invite our neighborhood kids in

We'd play our own music
And dance all night

Apt #214
Where the bay-bay kids unite

When them gunshots rang
We all knew the routine

Hugged up on the kitchen floor
Holding hands while
Shaken to our core

Once the sirens started to ring
We all knew the routine

Finally, air to breathe
We are relieved to be alright

Ain't it sad,
How us kids,
Learned to play
Around gun fight?

REFLECTIVE WRITING ACTIVITY

Were you ever raised in a city that was surrounded by either violence, drugs, and/or poverty? If so, how has this experience impacted you?

Reflect on the questions above.

"PERSONAL GROWTH AND DEVELOPMENT ARE IMPORTANT TO ME"

Inhale deeply. Exhale slowly. Now say the line above

Repeat 4x

"STREET LIGHTS"

It's all fun & games
when we'd play outside
Flag football
soccer
Tag
or racing on our bikes

we are all laughing and bonding
in some of the most beautiful weather

sweaty and stanky
we smell "like outside"

The sun drops faster & faster
and soon enough
No one speaks

We immediately hop on our bikes
run or walk with speed

Because we don't have a
timed curfew

so if someone asks us
"yo what time you gotta be home?
our answer was always ~~was~~

"WHEN them street
Lights come on"

Deziana
Torres

Street Lights

It's all fun and games
When we'd play outside

Flag football
Soccer
Tag
Racing our bikes

We are all laughing and bonding
In some of the most beautiful weather

Sweaty and stanky
We smell "*like outside*"

The sun drops faster and faster
And soon enough
No one speaks

We immediately hop on our bikes
Run or walk with speed

Because we don't have a timed curfew

So, if someone asks us
"*Yo, what time you gotta be home?*"

Our answer was always

"*When them street lights come on*"

Bootleg Movies

some kids will never know what
life was like with those bootleg movies

our connect stood out in the Walmart
parking lot off Davis street

~~nd~~ and yes, you'd see shadows of people
lingering

But, ~~for once~~,
~~For once,~~

A bonding activity our family was able to
afford

~~For that, we always would find normality in changing the world.~~

Do they even still sell them anymore?

thoughts writing Poem

*• crazy how we can find gratitude
in some of our darkest situations.
gonna start ~~practicing~~ ~~engaging~~ (reflecting) on
more moments of the joy I still
was able to experience.
even in the midst of hardship.

Bootleg Movies

Some kids will never know what life was like
With those bootleg movies

Our connect stood out in the Walmart parking lot
The one-off Davis Street

And yes,
You'd see shadows of people lingering

But, for once…
A bonding activity our family was able to afford

Bootleg movies.

Wait…
Do they still sell them anymore?
I need a plug
Still can't afford shit

Disciplined

Ever witness a friend's parent take off their belt
To discipline them in ways we all silently felt?

You stand and stare when their hand pulls back
Your body begins to move, you are fast to react

You dodge the hits, that were never made for you
And you forget to breathe; your body, now blue

You still flinch when the belt retrieves back
As if it were your body getting smacked…

The ability to feel one's pain
Is a gift in disguise, to reevaluate the shame

May you remember this when it comes to other's oppression
An ability to jump in without any hesitation

You recognize what it's like to be beaten
So, try to show up for others who are currently bleeding

Until we care about others' liberation
We will continue to live in a dehumanizing nation

REFLECTIVE WRITING ACTIVITY

What comes to mind with the following quote?
"*Oppression anywhere is a threat to justice everywhere*"- MLK

Reflect on the question above.

"IT'S OKAY TO SPEAK UP IF SOMEONE IS BEING TREATED UNFAIRLY"

Inhale deeply. Exhale slowly. Now say the line above
Repeat 4x

Disturbed Peace

Police come knocking on our door
They say we are *"disturbing the peace"*

With our music so loud
The one thing that brings us a sense,
of release

I wonder
Do they look in the mirror?

To see that the disturbance of our peace
May be a little clearer
If the reflection they see,
Is in fact the uniform of the police

Innocent people dying at the hands of abused
power is enough validation for us to feel empowered

A movement towards abolition
It's the only equitable, solution

It's deeper than just the people in the uniform but, the system in place that needs more than just reforming.

REFLECTIVE WRITING ACTIVITY

When people advocate to abolish the police, does any fear arise around this demand? Why? / Why not? What in your opinion is the role of the police? Do they serve in this way equally amongst all communities?

Reflect on the questions above.

"I MATTER TO SO MANY PEOPLE AND THEY MATTER TO ME"

Inhale deeply. Exhale slowly. Now say the line above
Repeat 4x

Fruitvale Station

Oscar grant's daughter begged
him not to leave the night he died
said she was scared of the sounds
~~[illegible]~~ of guns she heard outside
and he reasurred her that everything
will turn out just fine.

while on the bart, just hours before
he died

he danced to the lyrics ~~the song lyrics~~ ~~[illegible]~~ along
~~that of a popular Bay area song~~
~~everyone danced alongside him~~,
swaying side to side

"But I live like a rock star,
running from the cop cars"

~~[illegible]~~

Later, Oscar arant
was shot in the back while
handcuffed and laid out on the floor
By the cops he sang about, just right By
a death so tragic and painful
that even twelve years later,
we can't ignore

His death hit home for me
a real race war
it inspired me ~~to go no [illegible]~~
to save the hood, ~~[illegible]~~ something
I've sworn
How many deaths ~~[illegible]~~ will we Force
our mothers to mourn?

Alexa, play Feelin' myself by Mac Dre

*Fruitvale Station

Oscar Grant's daughter begged him
not to leave the night he died

Said she was scared of the sounds
of guns she heard outside

He reassured her
Everything will turnout just fine

While on Bart, just hours before he died
He danced to the lyrics
Swaying side to side

"But I live like a rock star
running from the cop cars"

Pop
Oscar Grant was shot in the back
While handcuffed on the floor
By the same cops he sang about just minutes
before

His death hit home for me
It inspired me to advocate for the hood,
Something I've sworn

How many more deaths will we force our mothers
to mourn before we find a solution?

I still can't walk with peace
Near the Fruitvale Bart Station

Joy Stealer

- Dezi Torres

Ever had someone bring up a good
memory of ya in the past?

Perhaps as kids?
Maybe in the pool on a hot summer day?
or at a park when ya got ya favorite
character ice-creams from the Paletero Man?

Memories that seem so fun & so unforgettable

yet, you can't recall
The memory for you doesn't exist,
so you continue with a fake nodd

"Oh yea, I remember now"
BUT, you don't
and that shit hurts

Trauma steals your good memories
keeps record of all the bad ones

like, ask me about anything traumatic
at any age
and I promise I'll ~~remem~~ remember even the
~~smallest~~ smallest detail

Because joy doesn't live in me
I have to fight everyday to feel it
and many others do too
you see, Trauma steals joy
It's one of the things it can do.

Joy Stealer

Ever had someone bring up a good memory of ya in
the past?

Perhaps as kids?
Maybe in the pool on a hot summer day?
Or at a park with friends?

Memories that seem so fun and so unforgettable

Yet, you can't recall

The memory doesn't exist for you
So, you continue with a fake nod

"Ohhhhhhh, yea I remember!!"
But, you don't
And that shit hurts

Trauma steals good memories
Keeps storage of all the bad ones

Ask me about anything traumatic at any age
And I promise you,
I'll remember even the smallest detail

Because joy doesn't live in me
I have to fight every day to feel it
And many others do too

You see,
Trauma steals joy
It's **one** of the things it can do

Passenger Seat

Calling shotgun came with unspoken privileges

When you sit up in that passenger seat,
You get rights to the aux
A bomb view of the scenery

But, have you ever noticed
When drivers begin to vent?

Confessing their secrets
or
Deepest suppressed emotions

They don't always need a response

Just a "*yes*" and a head nod

Its therapeutic…
Listening helps others heal

Remember that next time
You take that front seat deal

REFLECTIVE WRITING ACTIVITY

What's a good memory that involves you as either the driver or passenger of a similar scene? What was talked about? With who? How did that feel to express or listen?

Reflect on the questions above.

"I APPRECIATE MY LIFE AND EVERYONE IN IT"

Inhale deeply. Exhale slowly. Now say the line above.

Repeat 4x

Water Fights

Rember the days when we played outside?
HOT summer days when the homies would slide

Pots, cups, and plastic bowls
anything that held water
To pour onto our summer clothes

Uncles would even pop open fire hydrants
We'd hold hands to run through Them
our souls ~~will turn~~ changing from gray to vibrant

Most of us couldn't afford
entrance fees to water parks
and many of us never learned to swim
But,
none of that ever mattered

Blc on the faces of everyone around
could be seen,
with the most
Beautiful
Grins
:)

Deziana Tomes

Water Fights

Remember the days when we played outside?
Hot summer days when the homies would slide

Pots, cups, and plastic bowls
Anything that held water
To pour onto our summer clothes

Uncles would even pop open fire hydrants

We'd hold hands to run through them
Our souls changing
Gray to vibrant

Most of us couldn't afford water parks
And many of us never learned to swim

None of that ever mattered

On the faces of everyone around
Could be seen, with the most…
Beautiful
Grins

Splash!
We still wet!!

Scrappers & Cinderella Slippers

I'd close my eyes and pray every morning
for a candy Red scrapper

like the Bright cherry Red
Type color

I see myself in my early twenties
with rims so clean
aint no way I aint seen
man.
~~[illegible]~~

"i'm in The Building and I'm feeeling myself"
plays out my fancy grill speakers

A song That captures Oakland Natives'
attention, now we dancing ~~together~~
~~[illegible]~~
I prayed to be seen on my boss shit
not on my knees ~~working for a~~
~~[illegible]~~ ~~[illegible]~~ begging ~~for any opportunity~~
from the unfit

so, fuck the glass slipper, it didn't even
~~that even slipped off the~~ Fit Her
~~foot~~

I open my eyes,
shit feels ~~so Real~~ like a fucking DREAM

I'll take that candy red scrapper
over them ugly ass Cinderella slippers
yaaadaad FUCKING meaaaan
Hood tales > Fairy tales

Scrappers & Cinderella Slippers

I'd close my eyes and pray every morning
For a
Candy
Red
Scrapper

Like the bright cherry red type color
I see myself in my early twenties, with rims so clean

"I'M IN THE BUILDING
AND I'M FEELING MYSELF!"

Plays out my fancy, grill speakers

A song that captures Oakland natives' attention
Now we all dancing
Thizz faces and everything*

So, fuck the glass slipper
That shit didn't even fit her
I open my eyes
Shit feels like a fucking DREEAAAM

I'll take that
Candy
Red
Scrapper
Over them
Cinderella
Slippers

Yaaadaaaaaa FUCKING Meaaaaaaannnnnnn

Hood Tales > Fairy Tales

Even those with degrees stand behind barriers of oppression.

(Shout out to Aim, Ash, Jose, Kalii, & Kovoo)

EDUCATION

They say,

"Education is the key towards success."

Although semi- true,

It's an institution that

can also oppress.

WE DID IT!

26 years old
Five children

Four living
One angel

Single, alone
Pushed through

Family doubted
You believed

Painful sacrifices
Worth it

Look now mom,
We did it

In 2016, my siblings and I all graduated together. Loved the way my mom looked after realizing all her sacrifices were worth it. Single parents, please hang in there. There are rewards to the seeds you have planted.

Library Cards

(Inspired by Kalii Robinson)

They scan your blue library card
You now enter into spaces of
knowledge and wisdom

Books are in shelves; decorating the room

Some resting new, while others collect dust
All existing for us, to intentionally pick up

A connection to our past
A truth in stories,
Hidden from told history

When a book rests in your hands,

Who rushed to the rental card?
In a pocket in the front or back

You hoped to see a familiar name or date
Something like a sign from the universe to
Read this special book

Gravitated towards a sense of connection
The source lives around us

Read a book this week,
Visit your local and lonely library

REFLECTIVE WRITING ACTIVITY

The ability to read was something our ancestors had to fight for; it's quite liberating. What books have you read that may have impacted your connection to life or self? What did you learn?

Reflect on the questions above.

"I LOVE LEARNING NEW THINGS ABOUT MYSELF"

Inhale deeply. Exhale slowly. Now say the line above

Repeat 4x

Blue Jeans

In high school,
School clothes were something
We couldn't really afford

I had like three pairs of jeans
that I'd ever really worn

One pair was blue
With a heart I drew,
Blue pen stain on my right thigh

A boy noticed the jeans I wore
Just two days before

He gathered everyone's attention,

"Ya, she's hella dirty,
. She doesn't take baths.
Pay attention to the heart on her thigh,
she will wear them again, no lie"

I never, ever…
Wore those blue jeans with the blue heart again
My struggle was poverty, not hygiene

Next time you see someone with little,
Think twice, before you open your mouth to belittle

Damn, I really liked those blue jeans…

REFLECTIVE WRITING ACTIVITY

Have you ever been judged based on the clothing you wore? If so, how did that make you feel?

Reflect on the questions above.

"I HAVE ALL I NEED TO BE HAPPY"

Inhale deeply. Exhale slowly. Now say the line above

Repeat 4x

Goaaaaal!

When my foot touched the ball
I released suffocating anger

I'd kick with power,
Imagining the ball to be
The face of someone,
Who hurt me

Senior home game,
Playing Mid Defense
Rivals fight to defend against our
fast forwards with skills to aim and shoot

The ball is kicked far away from the goal
Slowly losing speed as it rolls right up to me

I stand at the half yard line
Taking a deep breath
Then I closed my eyes

Picturing the ball to be
The face of my depression

I kick with all I have in me
Aiming towards our front
Forwards to receive,
The crowd grows silent
Eyes flying with the ball
Above all players,
High into the sky

I watch in confidence
Speaking power into my reality

It glides just above the soccer net
Goalie doesn't even attempt to block
An impossible half yard line shot

Suddenly,
The crowd shouts in unison,
"Goooaaaaaaaallllll"

Remember,
Pain always turns into power

RECORDS SECTION
PASADENA POLICE
DEPARTMENT
MSW
CSUN
POLICE
BRUTALITY
MASS
INCARCERATION

Handcuffed

Under the 13th amendment
We have yet to be free

Black and Brown women and men
Unwillingly fulfill

"New" economic systems
Are really just us filling the pins

Label people who are marginalized
As "criminals"

Now,
When we speak up against police brutality
NO ONE, will listen

Handcuffed to oppression
Our freedom has yet to exist

They invite the oppressors with access to our school campus
Where they detain and criminalize us

Ever had to learn with your biggest fear watching you?

You want us to still be convinced,
That they are here for our safety?

We don't feel safe tho

Will anyone listen to us?

*Leave Our Schools

Metal detector screenings
When we walked through the school doors

Police officers watch outside of their cars
My stomach turns
Fear arises
We stand up straight
Waiting for our turn in line
At times forgetting to breathe

Handcuffing children as young as five
Placing youth in deadly choke holds,
As early as nine

An approach that impacts
Mental and physical health

Advocating safety yet,
Traumatizing many
still wonder,
Why we have high symptoms of P.T.S.D?

Good grades
Yet, they arrested us anyway

Who are we keeping safe?

I'm confused as a student,

Am I the criminal?

REFLECTIVE WRITING ACTIVITY

How did/do you feel with police presence on your campus? How did these experiences impact or enhance your learning?

Reflect on the questions above.

"MY LIFE HAS MEANING"

Inhale deeply. Exhale slowly. Now say the line above

Repeat 4x

Off Campus Lunch

Off campus lunch granted us freedom
To leave an institution
We'd experience some normalcy

In crutches
An injury from soccer,
I wave at the homies
That stood outside the famous pupusa spot

I'd see a car driving slowly
Full of men who wore colors
Outside of this block

"*RUN*!" I'd shout
As the shots rang, I stood frozen
To the advice I gave
But, couldn't take

Back to reality,
I drop to the ground
Metal crutches fell over me
I thought I was hit

Once cleared,
I'd get up
No victims of this drive by shooting
I sigh in relief

Then the school bells rings

Time for class!

...I MISS OFF CAMPUS LUNCH

72 Stairs

After class in Calvin Simmons
We'd walk up the block
Heading towards Harrington Ave

The stairs that were tall in height
Granting a view above the city,
You breathe a fresh breath of air

Then you look around
Kicking empty Mickey bottles
And cigarette buds

Realizing that people,
Find healing here too

We'd race up to the top
Competing for the fittest

Then would turn around to face
This beautiful, Oakland view

The dopest spot I swear

Man, I love me them

72 stairs

N0340

Sofia

To the girl who sat next to me
In Mr. McSwain's class
During the first day of school

The boys tried to get at us
And we both looked at each other

"They talking to you!!"
We'd exchange some laughs

Sofia,
You have been there for me
Through my darkest times

You never judged me
Never left my side

Now, sixteen years later
I am Laida bear's God-mother
You, her creator
Trust me with her entire life

You are more than my best-friend,
A blessing from the sky

I love you Sofia
You my mf ride or die!!

Brother Bear

My brother bear depended on me
His protector growing up

I would take an ass whooping for him
Would feed, clothe, and bathe him

I never meant to abandon him
When I left for college
It was never a goodbye

I realized my absence impacted him
When I packed my bags and watched him cry

He was too young at the time
to truly understand

I didn't choose college over him
Just desperate for a way out of all
We were forced to withstand

We barely had food
And money to keep a roof

It wasn't personal bro,
It's my hidden truth

Know that I cried too

Brother bear,

I'll **always** love and move for you

Just right before I left to college. This is the version of my brother I am speaking healing into. Love you Chi-Chi!

University

Straight into a 4-year university
I was proud

Struggles of the financial cost
& the sacrifice of not being with my family
Was really hard for me

First generation to attend
No blueprint map before me

Wanting to explore land untouched,
With knowledge not always accessible for us

Found myself instead wanting to quit
I often drowned myself in shame and guilt

I'd stay and swallow the pain
To become a version of myself
That everyone around me could gain

If I could do it all over again, would I?

Yes,
Only if society still lacked to provide equal access
And opportunities for my family and I,
To simply survive

Laundry

On move in day
During my first year at UC Davis
I was excited to meet new friends
In a city where no one knew me

In the dorm living room,
There on the brown coffee table
were a plate of cupcakes

Colorful and decorated with sprinkles
I immediately wanted one

And to the right was a young girl
Her skin color, white as snow
With blue eyes as clear as our colonized seas

Beautiful yet, triggering
Still I challenge my bias

"Want one?"
She asks….

I was hesitant to befriend this girl

Something about the sweet gesture of cupcakes
With colored sprinkles that
Played as minorities to the
White
Vanilla
Cream

She asked,
"Hey, are you Mexican?"

Excited to share my diverse background
I reply with a gentle smile

"*Yes, I am mixed with it* "

Before I can share
The blood that lives within me

She sighs in relief,

"Oh, so, you know how to do *laundry?*

Here is a picture of my family and I in the dorm living room the day we arrived to UC Davis.

REFLECTIVE WRITING ACTIVITY

What stood out the most from the last three poems for you? Did any memories of your own arise?

Reflect on the questions above

"I AM PROUD OF MYSELF FOR ALL OF MY VICTORIES"

Inhale deeply. Exhale slowly. Now say the line above

Repeat 4x

Street Smart

(Short Story)

New college friends
We walk to get something to eat

In the hot sun
I find myself struggling to adjust to this heat

We were getting to know each other
Before I heard the loud shots ring

Instantly ducked beside this red BMW
Waiting a couple seconds,
Listening for any sounds

Then instantly
I hit reality as the new friends I met,
Didn't. even… flinch

"Hey, are you ok?"
They look to me in confusion

Now processing it was instead a car's backfire,
I share,
"My bad I thought that shit was a gunshot"

They reply without any hesitation

"OMG, why would you think that?"
And
"Wait you heard a gunshot before?"

It was this moment that I realized
Why people with privilege never understood us…

They didn't understand the reality we faced daily
because their streets were safer

So, my PTSD like symptoms were unknown to those
that I was supposed to depend on

While this is true,
I still thought one final thing
During my overthinking that night

If that shit was a drive-by shooting,
I'd be the ONLY one

With the survival skills,
To stay alive

*Street & Book Smart

The Quad

A space full of grass

Students lounging around

Studying, reading books, or sun bathing

I'd walk by the Quad on my way to work or class

Free time didn't exist for me

I worked two jobs on campus

Also, a full-time student

I had trouble understanding how people are just free,

to exist and relax like this

I asked a friend who would lay out on the Quad daily

"How do you find time to relax? I need some tips."

She responds, *"My parents pay my rent and bills. Told told me to just focus on school"*

A tip, I admired

But, couldn't afford

Accent

Moved out the hood

Into cities of privilege and opportunity

My voice was uniquely "different"

Hit with questions like,

"*Where are you from*?"

Claiming East Oakland,

I was confronted with responses like,

"*Oh, no wonder! That explains your accent*"

"*What accent do I carry?*"

"*A ghetto one*"

Said with a smile tho

When we come into these spaces of higher education, you learn one BIG truth…

That even people with so much access to education,

Will continue to dehumanize you

I almost completely fully assimilated; losing pieces of myself to fit into spaces that were too small for me.

Code Switching

Taught a voice of professionalism
I learned to switch my tone and turn off my authenticity

A voice that came with
"Why you tryna sound White so bad?"
Whenever I went back home

A cultureless, fake sounding voice
More presentable and respected
In spaces I occupied but, didn't belong to

Code switching is a result of colonization
Depriving opportunities to exist as is

We are taught to let go of our accents, slang, and ways of naturally speaking

Then I wonder why in some roles of professionalism, I feel disconnected from myself

Encouraging people to hide true parts of themselves is misleading

So, why do we switch?

Are we afraid to exist as is?

HOOPZ (Pt.1)

My gold-plated hoopz
The size of a Basketball
$1 a pair
At the beauty supply store

Hoopz,
Haters would say
"The bigger the hoop, the bigger the hoe"
Other's stopped wearing them for this reason
Not me tho

Hoopz,
"Those earrings, are uh, unprofessional"
A professor provided a tip

My connection to my Oakland roots
Were stripped away after that comment

Forced to assimilate
In spaces that want my diversity
Yet, fail to uphold inclusivity

Hoopz,
I will never forget the day I allowed them
To rob me of my authenticity…

To put me in a box

That was never made for people like me

REFLECTIVE WRITING ACTIVITY

Do you find yourself code switching depending on the location and who is around? Why/ Why not?

.

Reflect on the questions above

"I DESERVE THE SAME RESPECT I GIVE OTHERS"

Inhale deeply. Exhale slowly. Now say the line above

Repeat 4x

Culture Suckers

What grade were you in when you realized school took away the most authentic parts of your existence?

What grade were you in when school was no longer fun but, deteriorating to your mental and physical health?

What grade were you in, when you learned about the history that made you hate your own skin and traditional cultures?

What grade were you in when you realized your passion didn't rest beneath oppressive institutions?

What grade were you in when laws passed to hide the genocides that killed off many of thy neighbors?

What grade were you in when you realized that although our ancestors fought for these spaces for us, that they still aren't FOR us?

What grade were you in when you realized that school sucked the life and culture out of you?

What did we really learn in school?

What do we need to unlearn?

Fremont High School Gym, 2009

*Protest

Death of Mike Brown
Crowds around campus

Traffic interrupted
Shouting “*Hands up! Don’t Shoot*”

We realize the problem,
Is deeper than we can see

A pickup truck slowly drives by
Three White students shout
“Fuck Black people, let the police kill them”
They drive away
The harm is done

Black people are murdered in the hands of oppressed power

It’s no secret
Although now recorded,
Seems like no one truly cares or listens

So, I march like my ancestors did
Against dehumanization

The war wasn’t finished
It only just begun

BLACK LIVES MATTER
Protest at UC Davis, 2014

College Confessions

- I never understood the big vocabulary words professors would use when they would teach in class
- It took me forever to read the assigned articles because I kept forgetting the words mid-way and didn't even understand what was being said (all five years)
- I would have to google almost every other word in my readings just to understand the message within it.
- YouTube was how I would re-teach myself something I didn't understand in class
- I would draw pictures, make up songs or raps just to remember the course material for the midterms/finals
- The parties were always lit
- I made some of my best-friends here
- Fell in love with a dope ass person who should have remained a friend instead of a lover
- I was on academic probation a couple times because I was unaware that I had a learning disability
- I wanted to drop out **all the time** because I felt like I didn't belong

Many people assume I am a perfect student, wanted to shed light that I too struggled to maintain my academic achievements.

REFLECTIVE WRITING ACTIVITY

What struggles did you face in education? How did they impact your ability to learn?

Reflect on the questions above

"I HAVE UNLIMITED POTENTIAL"

Inhale deeply. Exhale slowly. Now say the line above

Repeat 4x

Sacrifices

Although education has flaws

I'm thankful for all the experiences

Grandparents dangerously crossing borders

To plant their seeds in lands of opportunity

They are the reasons why I've experienced

Privilege and access today

Immigration in our nation is misunderstood and undervalued

To those who sacrificed for the next generations,

I'll forever honor you

Immigrants? Or natives to land?

REFLECTIVE WRITING ACTIVITY

If you come from a family of immigrants, what sacrifices have they made for the next generations? How have their sacrifices impacted/ benefited you?

Reflect on the questions above

"I AM BRAVE AND COURAGEOUS FOR TRYING"

Inhale deeply. Exhale slowly. Now say the line above

Repeat 4x

HOOPZ Pt. 2

In grad school
I promised to unlearn a lot
To not lose parts of myself in the process

For my school interview
I held my basketball sized hoopz in my hand
In admiration

That a girl like me, from a marginalized community
Was pursuing her Master's degree

And without hesitation,
I put them gold plated babies in the holes of my pierced ears
While walking right into that interview

Hoopz,
Powerful enough to stand out
And showcase my confidence
To show up in spaces
Unapologetically

Hoopz,
Don't ask me to take them off
For an image I can never connect with

Hoopz,
My roots are connected
I am representing

Take me as I am
Or don't take me at all

ADAPTABLE

In my MSW program,
They rarely empower voices

Seems like they silence the ones
That are often too loud

When you speak up,
They challenge **you**
Instead of any oppressive policies

They tell you to *"be adaptable"*

Adaptable to the oppression we came to disrupt?

As long as oppression continues to impact many
around us,
The work is not yet done

So, NO

I won't adapt,
I am not that adaptable with oppression

As a social worker,
If I forget that oppression lives in all systems,
I forget my true purpose

Was to come and learn ways to disrupt them

Grad photos: Authentic to my style and creativity.

Advocacy

(An email I sent over to a professor in my grad program)

"When we are in the field of social work, we must recognize the ways in which old policies may be oppressive to the students served. Especially students of color who already face so many barriers in higher education. This is what I am trying to highlight. Just because it's the way it's always been doesn't mean change can't occur to better accommodate their students. My hope was to challenge all to add more effort with students who speak up for help to receive that support.

The entire school knew what I was carrying and we were often silenced with no help. But as a whole, we stopped advocating when we heard "*there is nothing we can do*."

Where's the fight? The advocacy that you all preach?

We preach in this program that we can change systems of oppression and I can't even change my graduation status within the same department that understands the work we do; adaptation to oppression.

Have we lost faith in the power of our voices to speak up with things that just aren't right? Or am I the only one who is fearless in losing how people perceive me to fight against what is wrong?"

*Higher education is just as oppressive as many other institutions. May we always find power in our voice to speak up for ourselves and others

GIVE ME MY DEGREE

I showed up to class every day after my Sugga Mama died
Prolonging the mourning process because I needed this degree

I showed up to class every day during a global pandemic
Worrying about the deaths and financial struggles we faced as a family

I showed up to class every day emotionally drained and exhausted
Yet, providing therapy to students to reach my hours for my license

I showed up to class every day in the midst of a recent traumatic incident

Where the school was made aware and I had to beg to receive assistance

I showed up to class every day and continued to participate
Most times being a few of the only ones with energy to speak up

I showed up to class everyday fighting through zoom fatigue and lack of motivation

Due to upholding policies over people
I realized the real truth

That even an MSW program
Will fail to represent someone like you

I showed up every single time
In places they failed to meet me

Yet still,
I don't have my well-earned degree

They forgot that my personal statement
Mentioned that I am one who acts in the face of oppression

Trust,
No one after me will experience the repercussions
That policy holds over people

It's always people over policy for me

Now give me
My degree

*Wait, I never needed a piece of paper to heal souls anyways

Even those who pursue higher education, can get stuck behind borders of oppression. The fight ain't over yet tho, we ain't giving up!

REFLECTIVE WRITING ACTIVITY

Did any form of oppression exist within the school(s) you've attended? Describe any impacts/ benefits that resulted from this experience.

.

Reflect on the questions above

"I TRANSFORM EVERY CHALLENGE INTO VICTORY"

Inhale deeply. Exhale slowly. Now say the line above

Repeat 4x

I Have Some Questions!

(Who got answers?)

When did hate become more natural to give than love?
Why do we find pleasure in laughing about people's pain?
When did we decide to remain silent in the face of trouble?
Why do we think our voices aren't that powerful?

Do we truly believe that we aren't capable?

When did we learn to give up on our dreams?

Why do we have to work 2 or more jobs, just to fulfill our needs?

Do we not care about the land we plan to plant our seeds in?

Why do we bleed the same color as every other human yet, still refuse that there is only one race? (Human race)

Am I the only one that has some questions?

Forreal tho, who got answers

Silent Library

First day of grad school
I made friends
Rows of books
We sit at a table

We all have daddy issues
Except one
Bonded by trauma
We laugh

We Joke
Dark Humor
Makes it less painful

Hurting souls
With a passion
To heal the world

Social Workers,
Revolutionary
Turning pain into power

Unused Space

Professors tell students who talk too much in class,
to leave space for others

Then tells students who are hesitant to speak up, to
share their thoughts

Still, no one ever really does

Now the topic goes by without exchanged
perspectives

Silenced voices in class
Don't just need space

Guidance with tools
To speak without the fear of judgement
With confidence,
Power

Giving students the space
Means nothing,
If students are unfamiliar with
how to safely use it

Free game for teachers

Many souls confessed to me that they wish they could share their thoughts and challenge the perspectives they disagreed with in class. They admitted to being uncomfortable and didn't really feel safe to use the provided spaces to speak. How can we teach students to realize the power that rests in their voices?

MSW Graduation

Family surprised me in LA
Celebrating a BIG accomplishment

The first to pursue a Master Degree
But, it ain't all butterflies, you see

Upon their surprised visit,
I hold back tears that haven't been released yet
The pressures I carry are heavy and real

I share only the happy tears
Preventing truth from revealing itself

In ways that highlighted
This accomplishment was a hard and lonely one

That I missed them so much

That my school program stripped me of my excitement
When they left me fighting for the degree I worked hard to achieve

That during a pandemic, where I was forced to help other survive, I drowned

Truth is,
I am hurt and injured
Exhausted and barely breathing
Yet too afraid to admit to them

They see this as an achievement so historic

I take in the love that covers me from the painful reality

That I only mastered how to hide how I truly feel

I did it ya!
Class of 2021

Compared to my UC Davis Graduation photoshoot,
what differences do you recognize?

Rise Above

(My spoken word for my 2021 MSW Graduation Performance)

We are roses that grew out of dry and cracked
concrete pieces that exist in *"the land of opportunity"*

Coexisting in spaces of marginalization,
dehumanization, and systemic oppression

This sometimes feels like "home" for many of us...

Although these roses are born into spaces not
meant for growth, resilience, and power,
These concrete roses still find ways to attain it

We learn to wear these accomplishments like the
thorns that wrap around our stems to protect our very
existence.

Concrete roses,
You always find a way to rise above.

In this past year, we have found ways to rise above
a global pandemic
One that caused trials and tribulations for our
journeys as individuals and as students

Barely surviving through life, we were left
scavenging to be present for ourselves in ways that
seemed unrealistic

Sacrificing the peace, we desired so much in order to hold our roles as healers, liberators, and disruptors

Concrete roses, please remember to fight for your peace and to take time to heal your wounds before and during your battles.

We also showed up to class and internship after cases of painful racial injustice

Where other roses similar or different than us were roughly picked and mishandled in ways that stole the life from their leaves

Their fallen petals still decorate the concrete floors
in ways that stain pavements
with words like

"I CAN'T BREATHE" and "SOMEONE PLEASE REMEMBER TO FIGHT FOR ME!!"

You see,
Concrete roses are the toughest flowers, for they are the ones who witness life from perspectives that are often neglected and overlooked

Our vision is not broken,
The system in which you live in,
Is or is not

As systems are creatively designed to work as they do

Praying over those who found peace in the things found inside these corner stores

As colonization transitioned into slavery,
And slavery into the new Jim Crow

Where victims of mass incarceration,
immigration, police brutality, gentrification,
school to prison pipeline, and addictions,
are punished for depending on survival tactics to
endure the tough conditions

In addition,
Punished for attempting to find garden beds that
will provide the essential nutrients needed to feed
ourselves both mentally and physically

"The land of opportunity"
feels more like the "land of the colonized"

Despite these truths,
The skills and strengths our adversities taught us,
are what makes our influence in this world so
catastrophic, unique, and empowering

When we advocate against systems of oppression,
We break invisible barriers and chains that wraps
so tightly around us all

Our advocacy shines light upon areas of darkness
and lost hope

To speak up against oppression anywhere
plays as a tool to the justice we wish to see
everywhere

May schools remove existing and oppressive policies.

It's no coincidence that we all rose up from all we
experienced and continue to experience

For our very authentic existence is revolutionary in
itself

So, concrete roses,
We can't allow for our existence to sleep and grow
in a bed of lies and self-doubt

It will blind us to the reality of the power we all hold
to make the world a better place.

Yes, we have always been buried deep down into
these familiar beds of dry and cracked concrete
pieces,
But, they (systems of oppression)
Forgot that we were seeds
Planted with purpose

So concrete roses,

Never forget the power that rest within you,

For you have risen above many barriers
And today you have proven that planted seeds
In spaces of limitation
ALWAYS find ways to
RISE ABOVE

Power Lives in Our Blood

Power lives in our blood
Blood that carries the trauma our ancestors faced

Blood that shed from their bodies
As they found ways to become resilient
As they fought against the hidden agendas
of those in power

Empowering somehow
Ain't it?

How our blood is shed
Over and over
Again

Yet, new life
Continues to reappear?

Power has to live in our blood
Because despite it all,
We have yet,
To disappear

REFLECTIVE WRITING ACTIVITY

How do you embrace your authentic self, even if it looks different from what others expect? What challenges do you face (if any) in the midst of it?

Reflect on the questions above

"THE WORLD DESERVES MY AUTHENTIC HAPPINESS"

Inhale deeply. Exhale slowly. Now say the line above

Repeat 4x

Metal Detectors

Metal detectors exist in schools
Full of students like me and you

Don't believe me?

Visit those now gentrified schools

Are those same metal detectors,

There to protect them students too?

Fremont High School 2021

The entrance where our metal detectors were located.

Resistance

Granted permission to exist in spaces of
oppression, I realized one thing,

That although they tried to strip me of my
authenticity,
It was my superpower for my advocacy

The battle was big
My mind and body knew
I could conquer and resist

I fearlessly take up space
Where people like us don't really exist

Can't Comply

Comply to oppression
or
Sacrifice for liberation?

That, is the question

Taste my Name

I leave the taste of my name,
In places of oppression

Fearlessly speaking up
No matter the power or position

Not terrified of consequences

For the biggest changes today
Required some painful sacrifices

If you tasted my name,
You'll agree

That when I leave places of oppression,
My advocacy won't stop until
Those "freed"
Are really free

REFLECTIVE WRITING ACTIVITY

What is the origin of your name? What does your name mean to you?

Reflect on the questions above

"MY NAME IS POWERFUL, STRONG AND MEANINGFUL"

Inhale deeply. Exhale slowly. Now say the line above

Repeat 4x

LOVE

The beautiful yet, most painful experience in life.

Made with Love

My parents wanted to love in ways
That silenced their storms

Both witnessing destruction in families
Their hopes became just that

Kisses and hugs turned into
Fist fights and shrugs

Held hands turned
Into weapons of
Domestic violence

Witnessing
Abuse
Anger
And Arguments

As child
Always made me question…

Was I ever truly
Made with love?

Packed Bags

Packed bags
Sat on the front porch
Next to my light up shoes

He promised Six Flags this visitation
Time passes
Our seasons passes,
Never swiped for entry

He doesn't arrive

Decided to wait inside
I peek out the window blinds at night
Saying to myself,

"Maybe he forgot this time"

Mom arrives from work
Hurt to see us still waiting
We blame her
As the reason he left us

She remains silent
"One day you guys will learn to see"

Months later, he'd pop up again
Apologizing,
Hoping we are understandable

I forgave
And continued to forgive
He is the root
of my embarrassing
Abandonment issues

Her Reflection

As her oldest,
My existence played as a trigger
To her undealt with trauma

With a tongue that spoke
Fearlessly
I didn't just look like my mama,
I talked like her too

We'd bump heads
That lead to fist fights
During the late nights

Her battle with depression
Was enough to strip away affection
When it was much needed

Emotionally neglected
I became her everyday reflection
Of her biggest fears and failures

REFLECTIVE WRITING ACTIVITY

What was one time you remember feeling wronged as a child? How did you react? Has this affected you into adulthood? How?

"MY COMMITMENT TO MYSELF IS REAL"

Inhale deeply. Exhale slowly. Now say the line above

Repeat 4x

Raising a family

For years I've silently watched
A man full of excuses
Raise a family

A family that followed chores schedules
& Tasted his perfectly seasoned cooking

A man who helped with homework
And dropped the kids off to school

A man who would attempt to convince me
That his physical presence was always around

As if the treatment received was equal

A man raising bloodlines
Not belonging to his

A beautiful scene to witness,
Yet, hurtful too
I'd hate to admit

Didn't know it can hurt this much,
Watching my dad
Raising a family

That didn't include

ME

REFLECTIVE WRITING ACTIVITY

What is one moment you felt let down by a parent or guardian?

Reflect on the question above

"I KNOW REAL LOVE STARTS FROM WITHIN"

Inhale deeply. Exhale slowly. Now say the line above

Repeat 4x

First Love

A pastor's boy
A drummer

A great personality
Captured my attention

Started off sweet and catering
Before his insecurities drowned me

A life full of trauma
Surrounding the death of his mama
He struggles with both attachment and abandonment

On days my soul wanted to leave
He'd repeat things like

"Just leave me like my mama did"

A heart so big, he would use and abuse it

Staying to attend to his brokenness,
My peace, I'd soon lose it

*Blackmail

Leaving the abuser
I discovered peace
That didn't live within me

Ten plus years have passed
He still attempts to blackmail me

Fake accounts with nude pics of me
He is like a virus that
just… won't…. leave

Embedded in my memories
I was triggered by his existence

He'd track my location
Would beat on me
Kept me in isolation

Although I moved and lived
Miles away
He'd use his phone

And hold power to still
Contain and control me

What Did She Have?

In confrontation
With a man who just admitted to cheating

I ask the question no woman should
"What did she have that I didn't?"

A question that places our worth
In the hands of a deceitful man

An answer he gives
Holds enough value to impact my soul

He answers,
"Her titties were bigger than yours"

I'm convinced that men keep me in competition with other women

My insecurities are born again

I had to remind myself
of the things I did carry

What did she have that I didn't?
I'll **never** ask that question again

I am more than a body
A divine soul within

REFLECTIVE WRITING ACTIVITY

Have you ever blamed yourself or questioned your worth after being cheated on? If yes, how did it impact your ability to love and trust after?

Reflect on the questions above

"I AM MORE THAN MY BODY"

Inhale deeply. Exhale slowly. Now say the line above

Repeat 4x

Broken Records

Ever get into a relationship
with someone who filled the emptiness of
your soul?

Start off romantic and safe?
then as life rotates in cycles
something feels recognizable

you see inconsistent behaviors
that trigger painful melodies of your past

you feel unsafe and at home at the same time
It's also all you've ever known

Broken records are the tracks that reveal
Daddy issues and our unhealed soul
It plays,
A rhythm we stop to dance

Holding hands with ones you grant
chances too

Twirling you in their beds of lies
Bending you to break the hope that dies

Now covered in Rose petals
convinced of changes they'll never make
you sit in awe of the melody
that silently begins to play
BROKEN Records.
when will we learn that some things
ain't meant to be replayed?

Broken Records

Ever get into a relationship
With someone who filled the emptiness of your soul?

Start off romantic and safe?
Then as life rotates in cycles
Something feels recognizable

You see inconsistent behaviors
That trigger painful melodies of your past

You feel unsafe and at home at the same damn time
It's all you've ever known

Broken records are the tracks that reveal
My inner daddy issues and unhealed soul
It plays,
A rhythm I stop to dance

Holding hands with one I grant chances too
Twirling me in their bed of lies
Bending me to break the hope that dies

Now covered in rose petals
Convinced of changes he'll never make

You sit in awe, of the melody
That silently, begins to play

Broken records,
When will we learn, that some things,
Aren't meant to be replayed?

*Guns and Roses

Bonded by trauma
He tells me he loves me
Then pulls out a weapon
Aims it at my face

Eye to eye with the dark barrel
I fear not it…

I fear the man who stands behind it
The power he holds is dangerous

The smell of alcohol
Slipped his lips as he yelled in anger,
"SAY IT AGAIN!"

You see,
I made a hurtful
After months of no intimacy

"Your sex is wack"

Be very careful hurting a man's ego

A man's most prized possession,
Powerful enough to take your life

He handed me roses
As if they covered for the place of panic

I swallowed too much pride
Trying to stay alive

REFLECTIVE WRITING ACTIVITY

Have you ever experienced or witnessed any form of violence in a relationship? How has this impacted you?

Reflect on the questions above.

"I RELEASE WHAT NO LONGER SERVES ME"

Inhale deeply. Exhale slowly. Now say the line above

Repeat 4x

Tia Knew

Introduced to my family
I was nervous, yet excited

Puerto-Rican flag blowing in the wind
We arrive to my Tia Olga's house

We walk up to her gate
A male presence,
She can smell from a mile away

She smiles at him
Hands him a beer, and he takes
Later offers him a shot, and he doesn't hesitate

Now with hips swinging to the song "Brujeria" a Rican classic,
She asks for his hand to dance
He immediately grabs it

The aunt who doesn't trust men
Is smiling away and dancing the night away
With the man who has my complete attention

I smile in awe
Before she pulls me off to the side
Shakes her head in disappointment
"Playa," she whispers
And quickly I deny

But,
She lured him

Enticed him in ways that women typically tempt men
I realized his close relationship with sin

He not once looked to me
Or asked if I were okay

Tia knew,

A man's weakness with temptation

Wouldn't be enough to match my high vibration

What's Left in the Dark, Always Comes to Light

Hidden secrets kept me in the dark
Where light exposed truth to all around me

Upon introduction, she gave me this look
That definitely said something

Denial of a pre-existing situation-ships
His face of truth, I mistook

After about three years,
I befriended this woman

Invited her to our wild game nights
Confided in her during he and I's hardships

A friend,
A woman I learned to trust
Had a history of sleeping with my man whom fulfilled her
A bond of lust

And while we shared the room with all of my friends
It was a stranger that texted me instead

The message similarly read,

"I met you once, and you deserve to know,
that while all your friends smile in your face,
all of them know
That he and this girl had a sexual history.

So, let me take you out of your unknown misery.
Because they got you out here looking stupid.

Laughing at the fact that you are unaware
of the girl in your corner that plays cupid
To the beautiful love you think ya share"

I questioned him again
He confessed that long before us, it was in fact them

What's left in the dark always comes to light

Remember that next time,
You think you've deeply buried your lies

Done Begging

I Begged men for the bare minimum
catering to my emotional needs was
always one of them

Yet, I learned to stop being mad
at men who couldn't even begin
to love me in ways they didn't love
themselves

I chose incorrectly
I gotta hold myself accountable

B/c men who are emotionally unavailable
Have hearts that are ~~[illegible]~~
Unattainable

(I forgive myself for all
the times I begged.)

Done Begging

I begged men for the bare minimum

Catering to my emotional needs
Always was one of them

I learned to stop being mad at the men
Who couldn't even begin
To love me in ways
They didn't love themselves

I chose incorrectly
I gotta hold myself accountable

Men who are emotionally unavailable

Have hearts that are almost unattainable

FBI

I never understood why men
would lie
as if my FBI skills weren't expert
enough to discover the truth

and my team of investigators
were my home girls too
The NERVE to think you could ever
try me

Men, be careful lien in the faces of
women, who are intuitively connected
b/c intuition is NOT something
you can ever mess with

And women can't let that feeling go
Apart of our DNA, it's what ~~grants~~ allows
us to grow

So, instead of dying in the bed
of lies

STOP dating women with skills
like the FBI

See
everything
I feel everything
it's all energy

FBI

I never understood
Why men would lie

As if my FBI skills weren't expert enough
To discover the truth

My team of investigators
Were my home girls too

The nerve to think you could ever try me

Be very careful with the lies you tell

Those who are intuitively connected
We have an intuition that will constantly yell

Instead of dying in your bed of lies
Stop dating women
With skills like the FBI

REFLECTIVE WRITING ACTIVITY

Write a letter to an ex who hurt you. Express the things you never could tell them but, wish you had.

Reflect on the question above.

"I AM THANKFUL FOR THE LESSONS LEARNED"

Inhale deeply. Exhale slowly. Now say the line above

Repeat 4x

Love from a Woman

A love from a woman who has taken time to heal,
Is powerful

Love from a woman who is in love with herself,
Is deep

Love from a woman who admires and finds peace in
her insecurities,
Is courageous

A love from a woman can birth
Souls connected to internal peace

A love from a woman is unique

Don't believe me?

Just watch and see

Hear Me

Hear me out
I love the idea of love
Just terrified of it

My wounds of previous heart-break
Ached when memories would arise

To look someone in the eyes for six years
Then back to strangers, scares me

A love that is conditional is what I truly fear
Maybe ill try again next year ?

Can anyone else hear me?

Lost

I lost pieces of myself
In men who saw my light and used me

Who broke my heart
Apologized
Then continued to abuse me

Staying to fulfil the voids

Afraid to be lonely,
Existing comfortably,
In places of uncertainty

I'm lost....
Is it too late for anyone to find me?

THAT moment

Everyone has that moment
After years of forgiveness in a relationship,
And no changes
You can start to see a little clearer

That moment is a powerful one

Slowly detaching,
You leave when you are ready

My moment existed after he told me,

"You are a Latina with a bomb body, who after kids
will end up looking just like your family"

His way of motivating me to workout
Hurt me instead

Sacrificing my body to grant you opportunities
To have a baby with your last name

I left and never returned since

No matter how big or small an incident,

THAT moment,

When it happens,
Will change your life in an instant

REFLECTIVE WRITING ACTIVITY

If you are in a relationship that you know isn't for you, what makes it hard to leave? If you were able to leave, what was your breaking point?

Reflect on the questions above.

"I AM LOVE"

Inhale deeply. Exhale slowly. Now say the line above

Repeat 4x

My Ex Texted Me

10:38pm
My phone screen lights up
A new text notification
From a familiar name from my past

A name I haven't seen in a year
A soul I learned to live without

Wanting to "catch up"
Or to hang out as "friends"

It was then that I knew
He realized the faults on his end

It's been two long years since our break up
A year since I learned to detach my soul from his

Every night that year,
I cried and prayed for his return

Checking my phone with high hopes
To read what he literally just sent

Now before bed
Two years later,
I learned that I'm stuck in his head

Resting upon his mind
During reflection hours of the night

I am not the same woman
My existence, he won't recognize

A message I once craved,
Means nothing today

Even saying all the right things,
I desired more than he could ever bring

He will forever just be,
The ex that texted me

Who Gave you Permission

Who gave you permission to love me?

To enter parts of my mind, body, and soul

Who gave you permission to become apart of my identity?

One where without your presence, I am lifeless

Who gave you permission to cheat and lie?

Tell me, please tell me who gave you permission?

ME?

My lack of boundaries?

My instant forgiveness?

My fear of being lonely again?

I gave you permission?

Oh…. I see…

Love Costs Everything

I was willing to sacrifice everything for love

I will go lengths to maintain relationships with people
that do not satisfy my needs or expectations

People who do not feed my soul....

I stay because it's comfortable
I fear no one else would love me;
Convinced that my flaws are the reasons why

Once I sacrificed my peace, my sense of security,
and my worth to a man who couldn't even be faithful

To show my "strength" as a woman,
I'd forgive only to see that it played as access to
breaking me again and again

I became conditioned to think that giving up what
was intended for me to keep

Would instead cost me,
Every single thing

Who told you?

Who told you to love me?

I only love myself

REFLECTIVE WRITING ACTIVITY

What is your love language? How do you desire to feel love? Were these the same languages that you experienced while growing up?

Reflect on the questions above.

"I AM CREATING A LIFE THAT FEELS GOOD TO ME"

Inhale deeply. Exhale slowly. Now say the line above

Repeat 4x

Twin Flame

I met mine
A legit soul that knew me better than I knew myself

I loved him with a type of love that doesn't die
He loved me equally

No pressures to date
Nor engage in sexual activities
Existing freely in each other's company

Even our own toxicities
Can turn off the flames to those who match your existence

Twins, no more

Playing Games

I learned to not take love and men seriously

Dating two -three men at a time

With no intent to love

And yes, they'd know

But, to them I was the challenge they worked hard to attain

In reality, I was really about playing them games

Roles switched

Look at How You Found Me

You found me
Healed and at my peak,
Chasing more than the birds and bees

You found me
Finally experiencing
A sense of joy, and peace

You found me
Watched me closely from a distance

High in self-confidence and
Comfortable in loneliness
Makes me your biggest accomplishment

A queen,
One too emotionally expensive for your costs,

You enticed me with your attentiveness
Remembering the smallest details about me
That no one cares to remember

I fall for you
And you fall weak too

But, to the temptation of sin instead
Now I feel broken again

Because you painted a picture
of my dream life with you

And in the same breath spit upon it

As the thought of losing me
Wasn't enough to cost you

In the end,
I still win

Because look how you found me,

The woman I can still grow to be

Already lives and rests within me

One. Four. Three

(143: I LOVE YOU)

At the age of 28, that inner child of mine
Sat in my driver seat

Curious to the time,
Surprised the clock read, 1:43am

I looked over to my passenger side,
To the man who knew my soul
A truth, I just couldn't deny

His hands massaging my head
His heart big, bright, and red

A love song that can finally be applied
A person of peace, with energies aligned

One. Four. Three
Numbers so intentionally divine

(He is wearing my art work too, I could literally cry)

Be My Peace

My Place of peace lives within me
And in a relationship, it also lives within him

His soul; Captivating & Attentive

Gentle in ways that can carry me out
Of my darkest days

With him,
Guards are down

I am free to exist
and without fears,

I find myself loving…

Without the constant need
to resist

SELF-LOVE

The journey towards love where I thought it existed in everyone and everything else except,

myself.

The struggle many of us face, is the way we view ourselves vs. how society views us. Shout out to a youth detained in a juvenile hall, who donated this art piece to me.
Read her words and feel the weight it holds on her existence.

Now reflect on your own answers and the weight it holds on yours.

Who Am I?

At times I am certain
That I've discovered who I am

Then life hits unexpectedly
I’ve shed some skin

I’ve changed again,
Never fully confident
Constantly ever-changing

Who am I today?

Hopefully not the same person as yesterday

Yesterday is Not my Today

Today I am who I am

The mistakes I made yesterday
Will only reflect upon my character
If I choose to acknowledge and do better

So, it's that simple
But, I complicate it

Yesterday is not my today

Not unless I allow it

Mirrors,

My best friend during confident days
Where I find myself semi- obsessed
With my reflection

Opening my Snapchat and Instagram cameras
Finding random reasons
To record

Mirrors,

My worst enemy during insecure days
Where I focus on my flaws and fight myself
emotionally
It's draining,

But, truth is,
Both days only ONE thing changes…

How I woke up,
And decided to perceive myself

8/16/2017

Dear God,

I've reached a very familiar place in my life. I am again, insecure, depressed, doubtful and feeling really unmotivated. I've gained so much weight & I just want to figure out how to get up from it all. It's affecting my friendships, relationships, & overall goals in life.

Help me to be free of all this, & teach me to be confident in who I am and who I want to be. Thank you LORD, for allowing me to always trust in you!

I know you will help me be where I need to be.

♡ always

Dezi ♡

Photo Gallery

To all the photos sitting in my photo gallery,

I'm sorry for thinking I didn't look good enough in ANY of them to post

You were worthy to be shown off in every single one of them

Zebra Stripes

My first boyfriend had insecurities deeper than
what roots can touch

15 years later, I barely found healing around his
powerful words

"Why are you wearing a bikini?
Your zebra stripes are showing; cover your ass up"

I let a man's view of my stretchmarks
Kill my confidence for years

Words are powerful

But, words from people you "love?"

Impactful as fuck

Dear Deziana! 6/11/19
11:16am

You feel unworthy, ugly, and physically out of shape. you think that you have nothing to offer anyone. youre love language is words of affirmation because you constantly seek validation from others. you're so confused. [redacted] a man you fell for seemed different. His actions weren't matching his words so you decided to speak your demands and expectations and you haven't heard from him since. But again, you fell for someone who couldn't catch you. when you fell this time, it was harder to get out of. you feel numb. and dumb. But, your ability to love despite how much you have been through, is remarkable. you love like pain never existed. you bring life to lifeless souls. stop blaming yourself. learn to love all that makes you... <u>you</u>!

Nothing in all creation will ever be able to separate us from the love of God.

Rom. 8:39

Body is a Cage

(Inspired by Euphoria Episode 8)

My body is beautiful
The way it protects my soul

My hair, my boobs, my ass
Aren't up to societal standards
I sometimes admire them still

This body is a cage to the creativity that can flow but doesn't
My mind is full of thoughts like,

"You have to lose weight, you're getting fat"
"Your cheeks are puffy"
"Your ass is flat"
"Your fupa is showing"

Thoughts that never existed in me
That now transform the way I see myself

Here I am caged in a body,
A body that I don't love as much as I should
A body that keeps me chained to my insecurities and abandonment issues

I forget it is,
A body that also keeps me safe
A body that protects me against sickness
A body that restores itself after heart-break

A body deserving to be free
Free, from all this negativity
Caged yet, learning to be free

REFLECTIVE WRITING ACTIVITY

Why do you think maintaining confidence is a struggle in our society today?

Reflect on the question above

"MY BODY IS POWERFUL"

Inhale deeply. Exhale slowly. Now say the line above

Repeat 4x

Body Dysmorphia

Imagine waking up
Eyes piercing yourself in the mirror

Distorted view of yourself as three,
Maybe four times bigger

Your creative eyes play tricks
Your body, becomes your enemy

Loving yourself becomes harder
When complements play as triggers
To the beauty people claim you have

No matter what you do
You can never see what they see

And that's the biggest struggle
For the soul that painfully lives

Within,
Me

Enough This Morning

She looks in the mirror

Her reflection stares back

Desperate to feel love

Desiring to be accepted

Praying to be enough for herself this morning

The body smiles

The mind is clear from self-hatred today

The reflection feels free

Free to exist

Her reflection *always* hopes she feels enough this morning

Unaware

When will she would have this reaction

to her own beauty again?

REFLECTIVE WRITING ACTIVITY

When you look at yourself in the mirror, what do you automatically judge? Why? Next, look in the mirror and speak love and life upon those same parts every single night.

Reflect on the questions above

"I AM IN LOVE WITH ALL OF MY IMPERFECTIONS"

Inhale deeply. Exhale slowly. Now say the line above

Repeat 4x

Dear God, 5/23/18

today I woke up feeling lonely. I know I am surrounded by people I ♡ & who ♡ me. But, I'm just often times caught in a place of loneliness.

I know you did not call me to be insecure, so I give all these emotions to you.

I pray for guidance. I do not know the plans you have for me, But I trust in you

I also pray for all those who are struggling right now. allow them to have the courage to run for you before they run to the world!

Amen ♡

Dezi

May the Lord of peace Himself give you His peace at all times and in every situation.

2 Thess. 3:16

Two Choices

We are all presented with two choices everyday

Evolve or Repeat

Which did you choose today?

Clubs

The place I would go to build my ego
Spending hours on my appearance
To tease and tempt broken men
Into feeding my insecurities

Lipstick to cover my lying lips
When I whispered fake names
Into their ears of desperate men
Who easily fell into my traps

At my lowest,
Temptation was fun

♥Dear God ♥ Sept 27, 16

today I pray that you continue to teach me how to forgive. I do not want to spend another day allowing evil to control my emotions and feelings. I do not want anything to ever hold me back. My future has no room for my past. I know that my heart still hurts and that I sometimes want others around me (who hurt me) to hurt also. But, I know that is not what you want me to do. LORD, I know that you are never without a plan. Push me to pray for those who hurt me so that I may find peace. Teach me. guide me, show me, love me.

I want to forgive like you forgive.
I want to see the Good that you see. Challenge me!

Love always,
Dezi

The Girl She Was

She doesn't know
How she came to be like, this

How she ended up in this place of
Insecurity and sin

She only remembers the girl, she was

Bold and unapologetic
Calm and reflective
Confident and creative

A version of her that made her feel like she could
always conquer the world

Randomly,
This version of myself
Sleeps

Where did she go?

Restore your energy

Sit alone in a room
Be gentle with yourself

Radiate self-love

Fill the space with positive energy

Play music and feel the vibrations
Form a new frequency

Lay naked and vulnerable if needed
Don't feel ashamed or embarrassed about it
Learn the beauty that lives inside

Close your eyes and you will start to feel something immediately

Your aura changing
Your body creating a warmth that arises your soul to feel alive

Take a deep breath and embrace it all

Restore your energy

Flores

My flowers may drop petals

Reminding me why rain is necessary

Pardon me,
I ain't done blossoming

It's Ok

Who really has it all together?

No matter how much effort we put into planning out our lives,

It never looks the way we hoped

And it's okay

Grow from it anyways

Higher Self

I prayed for a higher version of myself
Resilient and Courageous

She inspires me to dig deeper and deeper every single day

She is more that what eyes can physically see
More than a soul can touch

She is aligned in her passion
In tune with self-love

She protects her peace
& no longer afraid to be lonely

Boundary setting Queen,

She now lives inside me

REFLECTIVE WRITING ACTIVITY

What are some small things you can do to practice self-love daily?

Reflect on the question above.

"I AM WORTHY OF LOVE AND AFFECTION"

Inhale deeply. Exhale slowly. Now say the line above

Repeat 4x

Grow and Glow

Grow from the rotten roots you were born into
Transform the pain into pressure

Find the beauty in nature and sunlight
Water yourself

Meditate over and over again

Live in the present
Not the worries of tomorrow

Watch your roots transform
From poison to passion

Plant seeds
From places of peace and forgiveness

Heal
It's your time to grow and glow

Dear God, Feb 9. 2017

I just want to thank you for all you have done for me thus far. Life is not always easy; however, with you, I find my strength. The greatest lesson I've learned from you was how to forgive. I've held on to hurt & painful memories that have prevented me from enjoying peace. I'm not perfect, but I do thank you for allowing me to trust you more than I've ever trusted anyone. Sometime, I am reminded of past pain & when I think about forgiveness, I remember to let go. Continue to guide me: where you lead, I <u>will</u> follow.

always Dezi

Glow Different

You glow differently when you begin to release all
that's kept you hostage

Healing is a forever investment
It's always necessary

There will be days where you are triggered

Experiencing mental breakdowns
Falling into episodes of depression

Still,
Find motivation and discipline
Past hurts no longer have to define you

That glow up hits different
When you learn to let go of the stuff that no longer
serves you

Who to Choose?

No longer at war with myself
I trust I have been through enough

So, I grant myself permission to exist
To feel
To touch
To be intuitive and sensitive

If I am ever faced to choose between myself and anything,
I will always choose me

Release

I release all doubt and insecurities about myself

For I am radiant
Shinning from the soul instead

Slowly discovering
That loving my body,
Was never a sin

I release what is no longer for me

Friends
Family
Jobs
Opportunities
Literally everything!

Untouched

Soul untouched

Many who ain't even met me

Say that they can feel this energy

From behind their phone screens

That has to mean something

Sensitive

I used to dislike being sensitive
I was convinced it made me weak

If you take away that single trait,
You take away the very essence of my being

You strip me from my consciousness,
My ability to empathize,
My intuition,
My creativity,
My deep appreciation for the simple things

My vivid inner soul is guided by how I feel

Being sensitive
Keeps me human
And connected to emotions
Others neglect to feel

Dear Deziana, ♥ June 7th, 2016

Girl you are soo strong.
Who would have ever thought
that you would be where you are today?
you faced difficult times. The hardest time of
your entire life... lost someone who was so
dear to your heart. But, look at you now,
about to graduate; got your own apartment,
single; free to live.. Deziana Inez Torres, girl,
you are so strong. No one has been able to
destroy you. No one dezi, so don't ever ever
for a sec, think that you are weak. You believe
and trust in a God who has blessed you time
and time again. Know that you fought as
hard as you could. Know that you gave everything
you could give. Know that you fought even in
prayer. Your prayers were heard Dezi; God has
bigger plans for you; so don't for a sec think
that something is wrong with you! you are so
Amazing, so loving, so giving, so forgiving, so faithful,
so beautiful, so peaceful, so everything. You have
so many women looking up to you. Never stop
showing them the correct way to heal.

♥ you girl. I Really do.

— Deziana T.

REFLECTIVE WRITING ACTIVITY

Write a letter to someone in your life that hurt your self-esteem. Express the things that you wish you had the chance to release.

Reflect on the questions above.

"I AM GOING TO GET OUT OF THIS STRONGER"

Inhale deeply. Exhale slowly. Now say the line above

Repeat 4x

Always a Light

When you live around what feels like complete
darkness
You get lost in it

You lose hope for light
You can't see any good anywhere

Everything seems to be against you
Nothing works in your favor

Consumed by darkness
You accept it

What you forget is that the light,
The one you seek for,
The one to lead you,

The one to protect you,
The one to bring you peace?
That light

Yea, it lives **inside** of you
Never left you
Nor neglected you

Where there is darkness,
There is always a light

REFLECTIVE WRITING ACTIVITY

Write a letter to your past self as your future self. What advice would you give to this version of yourself?

Reflect on the questions above

"I DESERVE TO BE PROUD OF MYSELF"

Inhale deeply. Exhale slowly. Now say the line above

Repeat 4x

A LETTER TO MY READERS

To those whose souls have been silently living in pain, I see you. To those who have been unmotivated, uninspired, and full of self-doubt, I hear you. To all those who want a life full of purpose, I BELIEVE in you.

Life is full of struggles and adversities that many do not feel safe to talk about. If this is the case, is not your fault that you suppress your emotions as somewhere in your upbringing, you might have learned that your feelings and emotions weren't of value. I hope that through this book, many can begin the healing process that is essential to our growth.

I noticed that many of us hide who we are truly are today because we carry shame and embarrassment around the struggles we endured. We are ashamed that our lives don't match what we see on T.V or social media and so on. That constant comparison will prevent us from aligning in our true purpose. You were never created to live, look, or exist as, anyone else on earth. We are uniquely different yet, we find ourselves pressured to mirror what we see in the world. Do we fear that what we carry inside and outside of us isn't enough? I challenge many to explore that more.

I appreciate you all for your investment in my book, and I know that one or many of you got something from it. I value your existence and wish you all the best on your journey towards healing.

If I can pass on any word of advice, it would be this line my Soccer Coach Teo would tell me. He'd say,

"In a world full of people who give up on you, NEVER give up on yourself"

Rest in Peace Coach

PEACE, LOVE, AND JOY ALWAYS,

DEZIANA TORRES

CONCLUSION

The Becoming of Her is a book about challenging and confronting trauma. In my experience towards healing, I realized it was time to pull back the rug that covered my hidden traumas and pain. I found creative ways to deal with each one and I provided a couple tools that you have seen in this book. Although they help, know that the journey is a long and forever one. Healing is a lifetime investment. One that <u>you must</u> remain consistent with because we all know, life really does surprises us with the biggest battles when we are not prepared. We will never be free from struggle but, we will learn how to experience peace in the midst of it. That's the overall goal.

In my entire twenty-eight years of living, I still fall short sometimes and I too have moments where it feels like I have to heal all over again. Other times, I think I healed from something and then a trigger comes up again and I still feel that same pain and that's okay. I learned to view the triggers as opportunities to reflect and heal more in those areas. Like everyone else, I am human too, and I'm still learning to be gentle with myself during the process of becoming "HER".

The best part about it all, is learning to become your own priority to honor yourself in ways you always deserved.

You all intentionally bought my book because you were interested in what I had to say and the experiences I was able to share. A young woman who grew up with a lot of trauma, is selling books sharing her painful experiences and people are buying it. You see? There IS power in our stories. So, speak authentically, write passionately, and exist as creatively as you can become.

Who you are right now, is more than enough

The Becoming of Her revealed my traumas and the impacts it made on the way I showed up or didn't show up for myself. This book illuminates the confrontation of traumas in different parts of my life in order to inspire others who can relate, to potentially confront their own. Through the use of the poetry, reflection activities, and breathing exercises, you were able to experience a glimpse of my tools used towards healing. Finding creative ways to release pain and to transform it into power, passion, and purpose is how I was able to become this version of myself currently.

What activities helps you to release a lot of what you carry inside? Does it help to release or distract? How we take care of ourselves matters when we face adversity.

The next books will focus on my healing from my childhood, experience in education, love, and self-love. These books will show examples of how I was able to heal and transform my views and perspectives on each one. My journey towards healing granted the ability for me to hold boundaries; my biggest blessing. My experience with peace today, is one everyone today can utilize as well. Holding ourselves accountable to unlearn a lot that was engraved into our minds since birth, is one of the toughest parts. Confronting trauma isn't easy. And I recommend all to speak to a professional therapist, if you have the opportunity.

In the next following pages, you will be able to find some self-care and reflection activities to assist with your mental health if you were triggered in any way reading through my poems. Please, this step is the most important one when fighting for your peace of mind. Mindfulness activities can be also located on over the internet, please find activities that help if these activities do not personally connect with you.

Self-care tips

1. Journaling

As an angry and deeply wounded young girl, I would watch my mama sit in her bed with eyes full of tears; releasing her pain onto paper in ways that allowed her to express without words to say. After, she would always be in a better mood. Something about writing and releasing pain made me interested. Soon after, she gifted me my first journal and together we began to reflect and heal from the traumas we experienced together. My mama and I's relationship used to be very toxic up until we both put in time and effort into healing our inner wounds. For that, I am forever grateful. Those who know my mama, will understand why I exist the way I do today.

In the book, you came across some of my personal journal entries, this is how my mama taught me how to express myself. Showing how I felt was raw and I know ya felt it when reading it.

For those interested in journaling, please follow the listed tips.

Materials needed:

1. Journal
2. Pen/Pencil/Marker/Etc.
3. Journal prompts/ Empowering Questions cards (found on Amazon, highly recommend) for guidance with writing if needed
4. Vibes Playlist/ Music (preferably something that gets you in your feelings or calms you while you are releasing)
5. Your consistent effort (because you love investing in yourself 😊).

Activity:

Find a private space where you can freely write and express yourself. Play your preferred playlist, set the mood (carefully light a candle(s), burn sage, or anything that is of value for you: saying prayers, etc.)

Take 2-5 minutes to engage in deep breathing activities. This helps to grant space to be realigned in the present.

Once completed, find a prompt if needed and begin to free-write. Do not worry about spelling, sentence structure, nothing more than just capturing your thoughts on paper. Recommend another breathing activity to close off this exercise.

As you are writing, recognize the emotions that come up and grant them permission to exist

Prompts to journal: Found on Google and Pinterest

1. Self-love prompts
2. Shadow-work prompts
3. Self-discovery prompts
4. Letters to self- prompts
5. Letters to others prompts
6. Past body image prompts
7. Or anything you would to write about

Music Recommendations: apple music or YouTube

1. Your own playlists
2. Lo-fi music (music with words are often less triggering)
3. Jazz music
4. Sound-bath/ meditation music

2. Meditation/ Deep-breathing activities

For an individual who experienced a lot of trauma, moments of peace and stillness never really existed for me. In fact, I would often find myself lost in my overthinking to the point where mid-day, I was exhausted from fighting through my own thoughts. I would even stay up passed 3:00am entertaining every possible idea and fear that entered into my mind. The inability to control my thoughts impacted the way I was able to function throughout the day. Impacting more than just my sleep, but my motivation, confidence, and ability to connect to myself.

In one of my classes in grad school taught by Dr. Paez, he would begin each class with these deep breathing activities. At first, I found it so awkward to remain silent in a room full of strangers and maybe it was just too vulnerable for me. I was someone who still had trust issues so, closing my eyes wasn't even an option. As time grew, I went from laughing in the awkwardness of silence to listening to all the crazy thoughts that would run by when I learned to remain quiet. With more practice in this activity, it helped me to focus on the way my stomach moved up and down as I would breathe which helped to silence those thoughts.

Guided meditations would also grant me the opportunity to get lost in words and imagery. I attempt to meditate daily now.

For anyone struggling with PTSD like symptoms, please consult with a professional if this method is safe for you. Sometimes silence is too triggering, and that's a normal experience so, be gentle with yourself. There are so many different and creative tools to help.

Breathing activities: All can be located on YouTube and some on other music platforms.

1. Box breathing
2. Shape breathing
3. Guided meditations
4. Chakra meditations (for alignment)
5. Sound bath/ singing bowls
6. Netflix: Guide to Meditation

Would highly recommend to start off your morning this way, and to engage in again before bed. In each breathing activity, the goal is to silence our mind and to not give attention to the random thoughts that try to invade our peace. As a result, you not only experience a moment of silence/peace, you also experience a connection to yourself.

3. Podcasts

One of the biggest tools towards my healing journey was listening to podcasts. Literally was inspired by the many voices who would create space for people like us to be validated and to be connected to tips/ advice that can be helpful. I look up podcast for inner child healing, for heart-break, for self-love, and so on. Encourage many to also listen to podcasts that you connect too. Instead of listening to music while in the car or gym, listen to podcasts instead.

Recommended apps to access podcast

1. Anchor
2. Apple podcasts
3. Google Podcast
4. Spotify

Recommended Podcasts to listen too

1. The Millennial Mija Podcast- Angela Aguirre
2. Do you f*cking mind- Alexis Fernandez
3. The Dream Life- Valeria Orsini
4. She's All Fat: A Fat Positive Podcast- Sophie Carter-Kahn
5. Healing Broken Trust in Your Marriage After Infidelity- Brad and Morgan Robinson

4. Connection to self

I learned one thing when visiting places like Hawaii and Puerto-Rico, I loved the peace of mind and clarity I was able to experience there. A real vacation; one free of worries and responsibilities. But, why do we convince ourselves that we have to travel out in order to experience that relaxation that we crave? Are we capable of experiencing the same peace here at home as well?

In my journey, spending time outside of the house and visiting places that surrounded nature helped me to catch my breath. In these places, I take my journal and/or great company and use the space to reconnect to myself and others.

Recommended places to visit

1. Parks
2. Hiking trails
3. Gardens
4. Beaches
5. Front yards/ backyards

Recommended activities

Encourage all to put their phones down during the following activities to avoid distractions

1. Self-help books
2. Listening to a podcast
3. Picnic with friends/ kids

4. Library
5. Deep breathing/ Meditation
6. Yoga/ Stretching

5. Daily Affirmations

I encourage all to engage in disrupting negative thoughts and replacing them with positive ones. During the book, I intentionally added affirmations to give all readers some practice. How did saying them out loud feel for you?

For me, it taught me to believe good things about myself that I never believed before. If you never tried it, it might be awkward and uncomfortable. You might feel like you are lying to yourself, I sure did. Remain consistent anyways, as they help to restore confidence, hope, and security.

How I use daily affirmations:

I write affirmations that connect to my soul down on a piece a paper. I practice affirmations by reading them every morning right after brushing my teeth. Taped on my bathroom mirror, I purposely place it in my face to engage with daily.

I also download apps that send me random affirmations around topics of my chose. I get them daily and each time I pause what I am doing to say them out loud.

Recommended Apple apps to access daily affirmations

1. **I AM** – Daily reminders pop up for stress and anxiety, happiness, gratitude, hard times, faith, work and career, and new beginnings. Costs might pop up, hit the cancel button to enjoy the free version)

2. **Affirm It-** Daily reminders pop up for self-love, body positivity, manifestation, growth, purpose and clarity, rewiring insecurities, healing, self-confidence, sense of self.

6. Reading is Fundamental

For many, reading may be a little, eh not something of your interest. Others may have triggering experiences from school that discouraged them to read. I get it. I found that for me, school turned the idea of reading into work that I did not want to engage in.

For others, books may excite you. What ever the case, I encourage that many feel empowered to read again. What helped me was joining book clubs or starting some with friends to read books that enlightened deep and reflective conversations. I can recommend some books that have helped me and books that are on my "to-read" list that were once recommended to me.

Promise me you'll try to read?

Books to read

1. Did You Know? You Are the Shit! – Jeremy Clark
2. The Mountain is You- Brianna Wiest
3. Ego is the Enemy- Ryan Holiday
4. The Four Agreements- Miguel Ruiz
5. Can't Hurt Me- David Goggins
6. The Alchemist- Paulo Coelho
7. Unwinding Anxiety- Judson Brewer
8. You are a Badass – Jen Sincero
9. Sacred Woman- Queen Afua
10. Dating with Purpose- Dr. Erica Holmes

ABOUT THE AUTHOR

Deziana Torres is a creative writer, artist, community healer, and social justice advocate who finds passion in the topic of healing. Growing up surrounded by trauma in the household and also in her community, she realized the impacts these experiences can hold on an individual's mental and physical health. Through the use of storytelling, she bridges opportunities for others find power in the pain that might also consume them.

Deziana Torres is a board member for Hood Liberation; an organization that aims to advocate for the hood while also holding space for community members to unite and fight back against the oppression that surrounds us. Follow Hood Liberation on Instagram @hoodliberation. She is also a board member for Healer's Coalition; an upcoming organization created to combat hurtful stereotypes through the creative use of storytelling. Please be on the lookout for the opportunities that will arise from such advocacy.

Find her on Instagram at @Confi_dez or her website Www.dezianatorres.com

Made in the USA
Las Vegas, NV
24 February 2026

42573534R00144